C000047870

SWEET ANAESTHETIST

JAY WHITTAKER

Cinnamon Press
:: small miracles from distinctive voices ::

Published by Cinnamon Press
Meirion House
Tanygrisiau
Blaenau Ffestiniog
Gwynedd, LL41 3SU
www.cinnamonpress.com

The right of Jay Whittaker to be identified as author of this work has been asserted by her in accordance with the Copyright, Designs and Patent Act, 1988. Copyright © 2020 Jay Whittaker. ISBN: 978-1-78864-083-1

British Library Cataloguing in Publication Data. A CIP record for this book can be obtained from the British Library.

Designed and typeset in Palatino by Cinnamon Press.

Cover design by Adam Craig © Adam Craig.

Cinnamon Press is represented in the UK by Inpress Ltd and in Wales by the Books Council of Wales.

Acknowledgements

Earlier versions of some of these poems have previously been published. Thank you to the editors of *Abridged 404, Atrium, The Butcher's Dog, Coast to Coast to Coast, Envoi, The Fenland Reed, Gutter, The Interpreter's House, Nitrogen House, Northwords Now, Poetry Birmingham Literary Journal, Poetry Salzburg Review, Sinister Wisdom, Shooter, The North,* and *Three Drops from a Cauldron.*

Not this again and *Mausoleum* were first published in *We Were Always Here,* 404 Ink, 2019. *After referendum results, I unfollow a Facebook friend* was commended in the Verve Poetry Prize, 2018 and was first published in *Closed gates or open arms,* Verve Poetry Press, 2019. *Old honey* was published in *The Last* (Lanterne Rouge) anthology, 2019. *Leaving* was published in *Islands & Sea,* Scottish Writers' Centre, 2019.

Provocation, The institutional writers, Not here and *Fragment* were written for the Scottish Feminist Judgments Project and were first published in *Scottish Feminist Judgments: (Re)Creating Law from the Outside In.* Hart, 2019.

Amelia's Bones and *Wasted* were commissioned by Ricky Monahan Brown for the Interrobang?! event Live and let die, 2018.

At the new pool was longlisted in Mslexia competition, 2018, *Who would be the ink* was shortlisted in the Second Light Live competition, 2018 and *Decorations* was longlisted in the Fish Poetry Prize, 2018.

Thank you ... to the community of poets that is The Other Writers, and to the staff of Fountainbridge Library, Edinburgh, where we meet; to Roselle Angwin & to everyone I have met on retreat on Iona—many poems in this book were conceived there; to Jane McKie for her careful reading; to Sharon Cowan, Chloe Kennedy, Vanessa Munro and Jill Kennedy-McNeill for creating the SFJP, and bringing together such an inspiring group of lawyers and creative folk, including the composer Ali Burns, who set *Fragment* to a four-part vocal score; to all my friends and supporters; to Jan, Adam and the crew at Cinnamon Press.

While I was working on the poems that form this collection, my debut collection *Wristwatch* won a Saltire Society literary award. I am very grateful to the judges and the Society for this support.

For her belief in my writing and for her support, I thank my partner, Marie. This collection is dedicated to her.

Contents

For Marie

Sweet Anaesthetist

Grandmother speaks

I was raised in a frontier town
by women who did their best
to prepare me for the world.
They didn't know who they harboured.

I couldn't disguise my canine teeth,
had to lope away one day
before I ripped them all to shreds
for which, I knew, I'd be shot.

Mothering Sunday with Gertrude Stein

I filled her   belly
coming out   below
slippery   bellow
head-first   out out

kaleidoscope cascade
opening vortex

cut that cord
can't cut it soon enough

Tank life

Only blood vessels, a pulsing heart,
reveal the shrimp, a tiny translucence,
spindly legs clinging to any plastic castle

peeking from upward-drifting fronds.

Not a safe place to grow.
Bigger fish speculate
on the next meal.

At the new pool

I was not popular.
The other kids ran ahead
left *specky four-eyes*

to memorise hard edges,
bench, clothes hooks,
the route to the foot wash

to tuck, snug inside my left shoe,
the coke-bottle ends
I called my glasses,

to pat my way, trailing
one hand for certainty
along chill, powder-blue tiles

to crouch, checking
where floor stopped
and water began.

This cavernous shimmer
thick with chlorine
had to be the pool.

Wah-wah-wah — a teacher's voice —
all the pink and brown eels
jumped in, leaving me

to stand, wondering
what I was supposed to do,
which was the deep end.

Jam rags

boys shouted
after girls
who'd started to bleed
school corridors echoed

jam rags, jam rags

they reached a hand
between our legs,
felt a wedge
of thick pad

jam rags, jam rags

terror of a red smear
on a plastic chair
surreptitious turning back
every time you stood
dread of stain
rusting your skirt
all the way home

jam rags jam rags

bloodied fingers
one foot on the laundry basket
struggling to find the angle.

Very important

She said
curling at the edges
very important.
Roll up, roll up
very important.
Be bilingual
very important.

I said
my corners, sawn off
very important.
Me, me, me, me
very important
Polly wants a cracker, no
thank you
very, very important.

She said
speak more
make friends
why don't you call them?
You should
make friends.
What do you do in your room?

I said
blend in. Head down.
My voice is all wrong.
Counsel of unspeech
my voice is wrong
    wrong
unsaying will take years

Radical

Where do you go when dictionaries fail,
omit you? At best, pathologise, smear you?

Kick open the rain-swollen door
to Mushroom Bookshop.
The bell's ding announces you,
thank God for steamed-up windows.
Inside, a friendly fug tinged
with tube-rose incense.
On every spare patch of wall
fliers and posters curl their corners:
demos, solidarity with the miners, Nicaragua,
buses to Greenham, meetings you never brave.

Skirt past Marxist theory, environmental issues,
past Black studies and animal rights
to the gender studies shelf
where lesbians and gays bleed into each other.
These are the days when B and T and +
have yet to fight their way out
and Q is still a dirty word.

To stand here and read -
the act of standing, the act of reading
declaring who and what you are,
seeking community, seeking common cause—

it's time to break from your cul-de-sac
overcooked meat and two veg
education to keep you in your place
hate blaring from TV and radio.
They can't mean you.

                    you're coming to see
the means of definition are owned by others
you were born into occupied territory
insurrection's needed
you haven't found the word for that yet, either.

Go to the margins. Keep flicking pages.
Eventually you'll crack open.

The mother is thriving now

The jar's throat choked
by a slippery disc of bacteria and yeast
that dangle strings, jelly-fish arms
adrift in dense kombucha suspension.

Flavour dependent on what it's fed
whether tea is green or black
sweetened with sugar or molasses,
how long it's left, ambient temperature,

how the household ferments,
all those hidden spores.

Scrabble deluxe

We played out our cold war manoeuvres:
UDM vs NUM. News of the Screws vs the Observer.
The wrongs of *The Voice of Reason*.
AIDS, all they deserved.

No matter what insults already slung
over mince on toast, Mother's Pride spread with marg,
tinned peaches—three generations would sit back down
at the same table, at the four sides of the board,

a different battlefield. Count out your seven tiles,
hoping to lay down a triple word score,
a seven-letter word that would silence the rest.
That would show 'em.
                              Quim. Lionize. Despair.

This was my home too

You scratch your scalp, shed
your legs chafe, shed
careless scrapings, cast-off keratin,
leached sweat, minuscule trails
all the specks beneath your notice.

I eat your clothes,
or favourite teddy

by the time you see me
I've moved on, no longer larval
cocoon outgrown.

As moth, I fold silver mottle tight
across my narrow back.
Startle me, I flutter,
speckle walls, ceiling.

You judge me for finding
a meal in my youth, swat at me
as though eradicating my type
might slow your disintegration.

Glimmering girl

Hooked at mouth's roof
yanked from water

thrashing, writhing
I don't remember the earth

or my slow, shuddered gasps
rather the upswell

crowding out fishsense
scales peeling from me.

I stood, woman-shaped,
said his name and fled.

Icarus in suburbia

Agitated flapping in the flue,
stuttered, stopped.
My parents fitted a cowl.
They were well-meaning.

When sparrows smacked
into the picture window
we waited inside to see
if they were stunned or dead.
Later we heard the scrape
of shovel against slab,
fragile corpses lifted
to the outside bin.

From our strip of over-mowed grass
pied wagtails skittered skywards,
perching briefly on the creosote fence
behind which we sometimes saw
the neighbour's football rise and fall,
rise and fall.

That blackbird hopping
through my open window
the flap of it,
shit everywhere,
its terror,
the scream I couldn't contain -

even so, I knew what to do
found a towel
to throw over the bird.
Its stillness, terrifying
and a relief.

At the window I flung it free,
watched it flare up to the sun
out-stretched wing-span
searing my retinas.

In my guano-splattered bed,
a single black feather.
My invitation to fly.

A knuckle of knot

It's a clean feeling
not to have fraying ends,
to be mistaken for a stone
worthy of beachcombing.
Taut with fibre, riven
from my mooring
bound in on myself—

a freedom of sorts
from the task of being
strung between poles
or against a boat's side
holding buoys tight.

Sighting

Once you've seen dolphins in Iona Sound
every wave's crest might be one
nosing the air, twisting white belly
diving, a delicious flourish of tail.
That's the thing about possibility.
You have to know it's there.

Early morning call

Two greylags sashay the shallows
rolling like broad-hipped women.
One seeks morsels, bill sand-wards,
the other's neck cranes, honk-honking.

Two more birds melt from rocks,
unruffling feathers with a shake
that same stately, side-to-side gait
in progress towards the shimmer.

They slide in, awkwardness gone,
bobbing, lost, among boats and buoys.
A life between land, water and sky:
I want to change my element.

Cowrie

The size and colour
of my pinky fingernail
serrated lips punctuated
by one speck of shell
if my fingers
were small enough
to prise it open
flick with my tongue-tip
till taut lips
loosen, open wide
tease, spell out its name
until the bottoming shudder
splits rocks to a cirrus sky.

Traigh an t-Suidhe

Sea-green gneiss, seamed
pink as dawn-tinged clouds,

every rock,
an undulating rumple

each crack lodging
minuscule dog whelk, periwinkle

clinging to ancient fissures
immense as grains of sand.

Embark

A packed case, sentry at the jetty's end,
ready for the inevitable closing of the circle.
However long I stay, there is always return.

This boat speeds me into brightening day.
On deck, I cannot find the phrasebook
for the language of home.

Landing

You have just touched down
in Face-the-music-land.

Local time, two minutes to midnight,
the temperature outside, cooling.

No-one holds up a card with your name.
Find your own way home.

Clothes you left strewn
on the bedroom floor

are still there. The fridge is full
of festering veg.

Time to make those calls
you would rather not make.

Where birds perch

Even from the bleakest concrete street
we hear dinosaurs sing, heartfelt,
as warmth and light drain from the day.

Gleam of an ancestor in each beady eye,
the same feather filaments, honeycomb bones,
quizzical head cocked, calling to us:

We too were mighty.
The price of survival? To shrink,
to trill unheeded warnings.

After referendum results I unfollow a Facebook friend

We had the same disease
growing in us, of us:
our cells feasted, gluttonous
on our innards, and we were oblivious.

Cankers grew in my breast
as in hers, were excised from mine
as they were from hers,
FEC-D and irradiated:
mine, hers.

Death so close.
They say each cancer is unique.
How else did we come to see
the world so differently?

A view from the Republic, 2017

The ghost of Roger Casement
is beating on the door

Driving west from Dublin
RTE fêtes the new Taoiseach,
pride at his parentage,
chewing over policies,
his choice of partner unremarkable.

We park at Banna Strand, a sweep
strewn with knots of seal-sized seaweed
storm-wrenched from the sea bed
and cradling broken granite.
History looks different again.

Meanwhile in London
imperial battles still rage:
who gets independence from where,
who calls who a terrorist,
the luxury of being an accuser.

Here, where Casement met his fate,
hung for principle and who he loved,
on sand land-mined by jellyfish,
a barefoot girl hops deftly
between opaque boobytraps.

Googling gorgons on the X25

I'm anonymous on the top deck.
Our fur-trimmed hoods, padded jackets,
insulate against the cold,
against each other, heads bowed
in devotion to glowing phones.

Once self-conscious pulling
Mythologies from my bag,
now I'm like everyone else,
sexting, swiping left,
tapping nonsense into my phone.

Back in the stacks

Threadbare boards press foxed pages,
held together by fraying cotton tape.
I close my eyes, inhale ripe book-dust
and here is my younger self,
librarian dilettante, striding
iron grilles behind the Round Reading Room,
latticed bookstacks curving above, below, a hive.
My privilege to wander in the cranium
of Western civilisation, keys at my waist,
sifting ossified knowledge
for the quiet, various certainties
buried in books.

However much I love these crumbling artifacts
let's not pretend it was easy to find anything.

Who would be the ink

cocooned in the cartridge
of a presidential pen
primed with iron gall
to preserve an autograph
that repeals laws
in the name of the unborn.

Passive, blue-black,
dragged through the pen
by capillary motion,
lying on the page,
your only resistance to choke
fissures below the nib.

Yet liquid is on the rise
flowing, as fluid will,
across borders
from melting floes
down the cheeks
of caged children.

Alarm

Waking, I recognise
(tinny, through a bedside speaker),
voices I quelled,
voices I put aside—
fruity establishment tones,
worried, workaday voices,
condemning us, debating us
as though we are abstract
not cowering in our beds.

A song for the small electricals

O broken wifi speaker
your champagne finish an irrelevance
now you are silent, unrepaired.

O epilator, jabbing and pecking
at my blotched legs, mechanical
witness to my part in this decadence,

take your place in the ranks
of small electricals, consigned
to a skip in the recycling centre.

O, the burden of your dismantling,
somewhere out of sight,
by someone other than me.

Daily disposables

There's a knack to removal,
a practised nip of forefinger and thumb
to pinch acuity from my eyes.
Overnight my contact lenses shrivel,
harden to brittle plastic.
These tiddlywinks,
slivers of Aegean blue,
accrue for recycling
in a jar under the sink.

Not this again

I assume we're invisible,
two women at fifty, plodding
through the heat, back to our car.

In my younger days I'd scan
the horizon more warily,
clock sunburnt men
clutching pints
ranged along the harbour wall,
their backs turned to boats
bobbing on the Solway.

Lezzies!

So many years
since anyone shouted abuse
it takes a while to register
late onset outrage
at a statement of fact.
Like we care
what they think.

Mausoleum

In the Playfair Library
someone has forgotten
to switch on the heating
and baby, it's cold inside.

From every ornate alcove,
blank marble eyes watch askance
as we shivering children of Enlightenment
are lectured on Brexit and data protection.

Peering at plaques on plinths,
we don't recognise these guardians
of a former order, their supercilious chins,
patrician togas, Victorian whiskers.

Reaching into bags for scarves,
pulling coats over our tailored work-wear,
it's chill as a morgue
under this splendid barrelled ceiling.

We could use some Empyrean fire
now we've made it
into the cadaverous ribcage
of the establishment.

Provocation

Ordinary wickedness
of heart
slapped her

reasonable frenzy
a mere man
lost control

claw hammer killer
precisely
struck her

brute retaliation
overwhelming
blunt force

facial bones
tooth sockets
act faithful

seven blows
act depraved
a disproportionate fidelity

The institutional writers

Leather bindings cloak
ancient texts, fading robes
no longer fashionable,
donned nonetheless
to warm old bones.

If we cast them aside
what will we do:
bury them, burn them?
They no longer suit us,
can't just be thrown away.

Not here

Not in this wall of words,
considered deliberations
of five judges, muffling
argument, convoluted phrases.

Not in the pathologist's report.
The facial injuries
the worst she'd ever seen.
Multiple comminuted fractures

Google it.
        Shudder.
                Look her up
find her smiling out of snaps
like any one of us.

Fragment

i.m. MM

Someone, somewhere,
wakes with something to tell her
aches with her absence.

Old honey

Behind the aromatic fug
of spices and vinegar
at the back of the kitchen cupboard

I find an ancient jar
of wildflower honey
still good to sweeten porridge.

A best-before date
from before she died.
Lid sticks. Inside,

paste granulates.
How many bees made this
and are no more.

The eye is the first circle

I'm mesmerised by Krasner's canvas,
an expanse suggesting leopard pelt,
leggiest spiders, feathers, dried blood,
four years' grief absorbed in its making.

On the facing gallery wall,
faded footage of her husband loops:
Pollock mixes sand, paint,
angles a tin to trail a slow drip
the extent of his wall-length work

just as Krasner spattered,
deliberate, his loss
on her grandest blank,
her paint dosed with grit and glass.

Amelia's bones

Women must try to do things as men have tried.
When they fail, their failure must be but a challenge to others.

Amelia Earhart, 1935

She's still making headlines,
new theories about her long-lost bones.

Eighty years since we first watched her
climb into her Elektra
confident, competent,
stashing make-up in the cockpit.

We covet that bloody-mindedness,
could use a shot of her ambition.

She vanished in Pacific Ocean shadows.
Radio signals glanced round the globe,
picked up by schoolgirls on shortwave sets -
plane down on a small island, half in water -

the world straining after her voice
we can't let go.

Souvenir of Craiglockhart Hydro

Owen will keep this sycamore leaf
riddled with black spot, tuck its serrated edge
in his breast pocket. A talisman
to press between a notebook's pages,
promise of a life after war,
when he might stand on Allermuir again
look down at Edinburgh's slate roofs,
startled each time how these skies soar
higher than Shropshire or France.
From the Pentlands he glimpses
the man he might yet become:
all the words he has yet to write.
This leaf will not be lost.

Wasted

Still the lurch
when *Back to black*
comes up on shuffle
Amy's voice riffing
our anguish on repeat

haven't too many of us
drunk ourselves to oblivion
shot up self-hate
our better selves passed out
on the kitchen floor

it's not a done deal
doesn't have to end that way
trapped in the trope
of iconic dead women
the roll-call of first names

Birmingham, again

Between Smallbrook Queensway and Hill Street
a sink hole opens
           I plunge
aching to tell a dead woman
how the city reincarnated
multiple times since we left
           how it melts down,
reforms into the shape it needs now.
Cranes, crossing cranes.

From a bedroom on the 26th floor
I look down on Victorian civic pride,
pubs tiny as bugs, crouching between towers.
           Only I lived to remember
our shared history of this city
how we burst out brash
onto last century's vision for these streets,
where neon livened the grubbiest sign.
Always crossed cranes.

The brutalist collarbone still stands
its mould-laced concrete surely marked
for demolition. Each time
this city builds higher, masking
the promise of razed ground.

Decorations

1. Robin

Ceramic rendition, cartoon-plump,
hangs from red ribbon,
no quickness in its wire feet,
no slick-wet eye.

A live robin
hopping
in the house
foretells a death.

2. Ice drops

Glass tears from Helsinki's bitter dark,
wrapped in corrugated card
for the flight home, buried
in office clutter until the final clear-out.

Three slender reminders slice
winter light: holly green,
blue of sea on a frozen shore,
rust of dried blood.

3. Vintage bauble

Arbitrary survivor strung up:
a brittle silver shell,
glass crab apple, gnawed open
to flaunt spangled, cerise innards.

4. Tree

That first Christmas,
mere weeks after her incineration,
how to mark midwinter?

Fake tree planted in the bay window
raw insomniac days,
sparse glitter-sprayed branches

wired into a frosted trunk.
Celebrate the artificial
rather than the dead.

Return to Crovie

There wasn't much of hers I could keep to wear.
Our fancy-dress double-act riffed on difference -
Laurel & Hardy, Demis and Nana—
if outfits required hats, wigs, stick-on beards
so much the better.

Crovie's half mile of foreshore exposed
her struggle to breathe. My willingness
to push a barrow along the narrow track
only rubbed her nose in it.
The tumble of surf on rocks, so close,
it felt we were at sea.
Though we didn't know it, we were.
But, O, we sat to watch such sunsets.

Years after her death, dawn aflame,
I open a drawer of wool socks
that she bought but never wore.
Still springy from lack of use,
they cushion my day to the extent
I forget I wear them.

Dumpender

The wounded hill continues its healing,
quarried guts still exposed.

Can a volcanic laccolith
remember dynamite
blasting a precise pie-slice
from its mauve flank?

Does stone ache at all
at the anniversary of its cutting?

The Malleny yews

A weathered metal sign:
CLIPPINGS FROM TAXUS BACCATA
WERE COLLECTED TO MAKE CANCER MEDICATION

Within the walled garden
cacophonous caws and squawks
ricochet from tree to tree.

That first anniversary, raw with loss
half-poisoned by cytotoxins
(but everyone feels shit on docetaxel)

I stand among stout trunks -
a huddle of four yews
trimmed to form one canopy.

In deep shade I trace
the tussle of branches,
each needle a culmination,

unaware a synthetic version
of this tree's harvest will,
at my next dose, almost kill me.

*

Walk a few steps, sit.

A kaleidoscope—desiccating
leaves, branches—filters
feeble September sun.

Walk a few steps, sit.

A peacock butterfly darts,
settles to feast on purple flowers,
splays mallow-blotched wings,

soars
lost against a cloud-scudded sky
dive-bombs me —

short-lived show of glory,
purposeful thorax
ethereal emissary

Yews walk you between worlds,
this physic garden a chrysalis,
a future hatching

I greet the messenger.
The veil is thin.
Or I'm off my face on taxanes.

Walk a few steps, sit.

*

It's my habit now to snap a sprig
stroke slender, skeletal needles,
wonder what would happen if I licked my fingers?

I don't feel this way
about bleach under the sink,
or paracetamol in a bedside drawer.

My sweet anaesthetist:
ancient poison growing among us.
One passage out of here.

Water's edge

Every path has two lives: one with,
one without you. Beyond furrowed fields
the farm's spine leans against sky.

As talisman, I choose a twig
the length of my hand, every knot
and twist of bark alive with moss.

How much more I see in silence:
a seam of carmine leaves
tracing the contours of the bank;

the steel of a heron's wing lifting
into air, as though it understood
being blown back on course.

Baggage

Your home, the one you made all by yourself,
after the last lover to leave
upped and went with only a suitcase.

Each leaving harks back to the first:
you, mewling at nuns in a Magdalen cot.
Your birth mother's loss,

yours too, now mine,
intricacies plaiting me
into a story started fifty years back.

My fierce, proud one,
step carefully over crimson afterbirth.
Dig it into the roses, the richest fertiliser.

Sleeping alone together

We shelter from the night, the world,
one quilted mound risen
in the shadow of an ancient hill,
a treasure horde to uncover.

We turn our backs
on former companions,
unkeepable troths,
widow's keening—

those were our lovers
and this is our love.
We are here, now. Only human
to remake the bed and weep.

Local knowledge

East Lothian oaks, transplanted
from French estates,
conceal a cache of truffles
for those who know where to look.

As for Hailes castle,
Bothwell's birthplace,
more residence than fortress,
marital problems quoth an info-board—

you told me
there was a porno shoot here
hard to imagine anything
but goosebumps.

In the flightpath

Low over Brian and Irene's roof
a man-made mantis rises,
barbed head hooking the sky.
Twin engines blaze furnace-red.

I am nothing but turbulent water,
wholly vibration, tracking the throb
from Traprain to Berwick Law
each cell juddered to its core.

*

Twelve bees drowse on the lavender.
Swifts swirl, swoop, startled
into formation over fields
of tatties and broad beans.

My smartphone tells me
this cocky Eurofighter,
circling East Lothian
for public spectacle,

proved its worth
in active combat in Syria.
Imagine cowering in bed.
Imagine your children crying.

Seafaring

When I step away, my darling,
it's only to look
through another window, to revel
briefly in another sky
where birds chatter
in language I can't decipher.

At this stage in our voyage
the cargo we each freight
has need of different seas.
Patience. We are heading
for the same port.
I am sure of that.

Funnel web

The trap made visible:
scraps of glistening gauze
stretch over grass to dry.

Each netted skein of silk
cradles droplets,
dazzling mercury beads.

A deep plunge holds
the spider's hopes.

Glioblastoma

i.m. FM

Hard to know, in these times,
what we wake to.
Today, east coast haar
muffles tenements and spires.

The sun is still struggling
to burn through mist,
lying low, remembering
how it backlit May leaves,
flaring heart intact.

Snagged in branches,
a kite ribbon flutters -
glorious orange
whether the sky is sharpest blue
or softest grey.

Eyrie

101 metres above Iona, seeking signal on Dun Í—no bars. I stab numb fingers on the shiny screen for updates that would be unreadable in the reflected glare. Gusts bully me into zipping the phone away. Have some respect. Look. Stare to middle distance: tractors trundle silage to cows, and beyond, the sea beats serried gneiss into pebbles. I need both hands to hold on, won't be prised from this crevice. Think barnacles, limpets. Know the wind as tide, to be endured, scouring my face. Clouds scroll over the north island, until, fleeting as thought,

sliver of shadow skims,
hearts catch—all eyes lift to sea-eagle,
those slow, scything wing beats.

It circles the crags, surveying us all: walkers, pilgrims, Hebridean ewes and lambs, wary greylag geese. Smaller birds shriek alarm. And I imagine her, hundreds of miles south, shaken, nursing this latest diagnosis, bursting from low-ceiling consulting rooms, past waiting ranks of barely-contained fidgeters, trapped under strip-light, inhaling that clinical smell.

May her eagle-sense
swoop with raptor's precision,
snatch every morsel.

Back in the waiting room

Another fork in the road.
One route loops back to needles,
bad news, pain. The other stretches
to foothills; its end hidden
under low-lying mist.

Truth is, we're already set on a path.
Our bodies have already chosen to blossom,
wither in their own season.
Eyes, don't register what's ahead,
feet, keep on walking.

Elective

I'm asked to consider *a loss of fertility*
(at 51, childless, five years a crone),
asked to consider *menopause*
(I've already sweated that, thanks).

I choose to excise what cannot be fixed,
chop out statistical likelihoods,
ready to bluff a few more hands—
I learned pontoon from a pessimist.

I offer my wrist to the anaesthetist,
my ovaries to the pathologist,
a juicy cyst for the surgeon to burst.
The rest, to the bucket incinerator.

Sweet anaesthetist

His role: to shepherd me
to transcendence,
drown me in brackish stupor.

Efficient appraisal of my open
mouth, dry from fasting,
A difficult airway

drumming hard on the back
of my hand, his fingers raise veins
where others failed.

He guarantees obliteration,
yet reminds me
of an old friend, a gentle man

whose name I forget
as I sag, rag-doll limp,
thoughts clotting

Dark moon, midwinter

We step into a muted world.
Night wicks the grass grey,

streetlights nibble a fuzzy edge
around the park's obsidian heart.

I've never understood
why we're supposed to be afraid.

Egg case

My left ovary is smothered in seven centimetres of cyst. A risk to be reduced.

—#—

A beachcombed husk in my palm, multiple crumpled chambers deflated and dried, bereft of hatched whelks. A self-contained nodule of nothing, pod of naught.

—#—

Wobbling on a wooden stool in the school biology lab, I clench my sharpened pencil, transcribe the handbag and curved horns into my exercise book. I will keep practising until fluent, ready to reproduce constituent parts in cartoonish simplicity -

a handbag and curved horns.

I lay my transparent ruler across the paper and draw straight lines, and label (best handwriting): Ovaries, Ampulla, Endometrium, Fallopian Tubes.

But I don't know them. Not viscerally.

—#—

And how much less interesting than the febrile atmosphere in the school hall on the day one hundred twelve year olds are herded in to watch *the childbirth video*.

At the crowning, commotion at the front. The boy who faints will be taunted for years.

—#—

Imagine: my abdomen crammed with congealed jelly babies.

—#—

Sometimes I looked up and my mother was watching me, as though wondering what she'd done.

—#—

My mother tells me:

It was the bloody ants' fault. I was pregnant with you. Your father was away. You know how I hate ants in the house.

—#—

I am possible.

—#—

Inexorable ant-march across a kitchen floor. No-one to talk her down or reassure. Scrubbing. Safe to use ant powder inside, when pregnant? Not sure. Read and reread the packet. Relentless. Ants keep marching. Need to empty the cupboard under counter anyway, in case the ants find it, find the flour and sugar inside. Visions of a never-ending ant-army carrying their sugar lumps aloft, victorious, back to their queen.

Lifting and bending—getting up and down—panicking about ants and—wet in her knickers—a pooling. Blood—

I am choosing

A punishment for leaving it so late to have a child. For thinking, in their cleverness, with their science, they were above this. The thought of her mother's told-you-so triumph.

—#—

The GP said his wife took these tablets too; I would never have taken anything when I was pregnant, I even stopped smoking, I was so careful but I thought I was miscarrying—

A risk reduced.

I am possible.

—#—

Alone in bed, sleepless, praying to the god her husband denies.

—#—

She tells me when I am eighteen, have left home for a University ninety miles north, *It was in the Sunday Times a few years after you were born. All the cancers in the daughters are at puberty; you're safe.* She tells me now *because of course you maybe shouldn't go on the pill.*

I am already on the pill.

She tells me in such a way that makes it clear we won't talk about it again.

—#—

A hunt for the untold, the unnamed. In the Science Library, I turn the handle on a microfilm reader, not too fast (nausea). Oestrogen. Estrogen. Diethylstilboestrol. Diethylstilbestrol. Stilbestrol. DES. Leading me to the long shelves of *Index Medicus*, metres of cloth-bound volumes, to rifle bible-thin paper.

I school myself in libraries, their tools, fiche readers, bibliographies, catalogues, all they contain. All that was withheld. All that was never vocalised.

All the swallowed words.

—#—

My inheritance:

Great grandfather—dies of sarcoma.

Grandmother—dies of breast cancer.

Mother—exposure to DES in pregnancy. Two breast cancers. Dies of ovarian cancer.

Me—exposure to DES *in utero*. One breast cancer (and counting).

I am choosing.

—#—

Buried deep in my pelvis and scheduled for excision: tissue, but more than tissue. My snail shells, my coiled snakes. Mysterious, seen on scans, analysed by faceless medics, discussed in front of me in medical language by my partner and my consultant, doctor to doctor—I have no clue, really.

I am excising a possibility.

—#—

Absence is a poke of pain when I bend forward too quickly, a stabbing gyroscope, a whirligig of knife-ache when I lie on my left side.

—#—

A risk reduced.

Intrinsic

All I know
is there's a word
I've forgotten

I falter.
Tongue stalls,
loading ...

Everyone stares

and my lost word
damns any flow

I flounder
splashing word-water
It begins with I...
It's when something is inside ...

Interlopers elbow to the front

integral   intellect
interned   integrity.

I am being stared at
as I do the shell
of my father, guttering
in his nursing home bed,
uttering aphasic nonsense.

Panic tastes metallic.

Does the motorway,
deserted at night,
pine for cars?

Does it relish
taut, empty tarmac?

Blame home-time on Fridays,
my age, medication -

Breathe.
Be a river surging
round this stone.
Let me flow.

Let *intrinsic* go.

Notes

Radical: Mushroom was Nottingham's radical bookshop between 1972 and 2000.

Glimmering girl was written in response to (and the title is a phrase from) WB Yeats's 'The Song of Wandering Aengus.'

Traigh an t-Suidhe is a beach on Iona.

Where birds perch: '…the Liaoning fossils confirm where birds perch on the dinosaur family tree. Birds are a type of theropod.' *The Rise and Fall of the Dinosaurs: The Untold Story of a Lost World* by Steve Brusatte, Pan Macmillan (2019), used with kind permission.

After Referendum results…: FEC-D is a standard chemotherapy for advanced breast cancer.

A view from the Republic, 2017: The epigram is from W.B Yeats' poem 'The Ghost of Roger Casement.'

Provocation, The institutional writers, Not here and Fragment were written in response to the case of Drury vs H.M. Advocate (2001) as part of the creative strand of the Scottish Feminist Judgements Project.
https://www.sfjp.law.ed.ac.uk/.
Drury was unanimously convicted of the murder of his ex-partner Marilyn McKenna, but not before the judge had ruled that it would be appropriate for the jury to consider a defence of 'provocation by sexual infidelity' which is (at time of writing) still admissible in Scotland. Provocation is a found poem using words from the deliberations of five judges.

The eye is the first circle: Pollock's wife, Lee Krasner, was so traumatised by his death that it was the 60s before she ceased wrestling with his powerful ghost.

Amelia's bones: Amelia Earhart, 1897-1937

Souvenir of Craiglockhart Hydro: Wilfred Owen's papers record his walks into the Pentland Hills from Craiglockhart War Hospital (formerly Hydro)where he was being treated for shell shock, during 1917.

Wasted: Amy Winehouse, 1983-2011.

The hill Dumpender, near East Linton in East Lothian, Scotland, is also known as Traprain Law.

The line 'sleeping alone together' is from 'To My Wife at Midnight' by W.S. Graham, included in *New Collected Poems* (Faber and Faber, 2004). Reproduced with permission from the estate of W.S. Graham. 'Sleeping alone together' was written in response to this poem.

Egg Case: Between the 1940s and the early 1970s the synthetic oestrogen known as diethylstilbestrol (DES) was given to (at a conservative estimate) 300,000 UK women who doctors believed were at an increased risk of miscarriage. Although in 1953 a clinical study found DES did nothing to reduce the risk of miscarriage, it was used until 1971, when it was found the daughters of women who took the drug were at increased risk of rare cancers of the vagina and the cervix. Further research subsequently linked DES to increased risk of breast cancer in mothers (and daughters).